Original title:
Rhododendron Revelry

Copyright © 2025 Creative Arts Management OÜ
All rights reserved.

Author: Alec Davenport
ISBN HARDBACK: 978-1-80567-016-2
ISBN PAPERBACK: 978-1-80567-096-4

Blossoms in a Whirl of Color

In the garden, colors clash,
Petals twirl in a crazy smash.
Bees don shades, buzzing with flair,
Their dance a riot, beyond compare.

Squirrels wear hats, strut with pride,
Diamonds made of dew, side by side.
Flowers chuckle with fragrant glee,
Nature's laughter, wild and free.

Petals Paint the Spring

Jellybeans tumble from trees so grand,
As bunnies dig in the rainbow land.
Colors spill like paint on the ground,
Every step a giggle, a sight unbound.

Umbrellas pop, as raindrops sing,
A waltz of joy, with each little thing.
Tulips give head nods all around,
In this silly show, so profound!

Whispers of the Mountain Bloom

Mountains chat, their gossip flows,
With petals blushing in nature's throes.
Breezes tease with a playful nudge,
Atop the hills, they dare to judge.

Butterflies pull pranks, oh so sly,
Chasing their shadows, making them fly.
Laughter bubbles from streams like wine,
Where blooms blend perfectly, divine.

Dance of the Vibrant Flora

Daisies twirl in their polka dot gowns,
While daisies stare with giggling frowns.
The wind picks up, the party's a blast,
As starlings swoop low, a colorful cast.

Laughing leaves join in the spree,
Tickling branches, wild and free.
In this garden, bright and spry,
Nature's a joker, reaching for the sky.

The Language of Blossoms

In the garden, blooms conspire,
Whispers sweet, they never tire.
Petals giggle in the breeze,
Talking secrets with the trees.

Colors clash like playful friends,
With their jokes, the laughter blends.
A rose slips on a silly hat,
While daisies dance with a comic cat.

Canvas of the Enchanted Garden

Spray-paint petals, bright and bold,
Nature's canvas, stories told.
Sunflowers wear their sunny grin,
While violets snicker, where to begin?

Laughter echoes on the vine,
Buds are plotting every line.
A gladiolus with a joke so new,
Makes lilacs chuckle, splitting the dew.

Where Petals Dance

In the meadow, flowers tease,
Twirl around with utmost ease.
Tulips tickle with their flair,
Carnations giggle in the air.

Butterflies join the frothy fun,
Waltzing 'neath the warming sun.
Hibiscus leaps with charms to share,
While lilies laugh without a care.

Whispers of the Floral Symphony

Petals whisper, oh so sly,
Giggling as the bees buzz by.
The marigold tells a funny tale,
While ferns chuckle without fail.

Cacti crack a prickly joke,
As poppies frolic, then they poke.
Each flower's planted for a laugh,
In this botanical photograph.

Petals Unfurled

In hues of pink and purple glow,
A tiny bee lost, what a show!
He buzzed around like he was dancing,
Whispering secrets, so entrancing.

With every bloom, a new surprise,
A frog jumped out, but oh, he's shy!
He croaked a tune to the blooming crowd,
In laughter, the flowers all felt proud.

In the Heart of Nature's Canvas

Where laughter paints the lively scene,
A squirrel twirls, oh so keen!
He juggles acorns with pure delight,
While birds chirp, taking flight.

The sun peeks in with a playful grin,
Knocking at petals, to let the fun begin.
A butterfly, in mismatched clothes,
Struts by, flaunting his colorful pose.

The Aromatic Odyssey

A fragrance wafts from flower to bee,
'Hey there, friend! Come dance with me!'
The breeze giggles, a soft embrace,
As petals shimmer in the sunny space.

A caterpillar crawls, munching away,
While planning his bright pupating day.
He's got dreams of wings and fancy flight,
Chasing rainbows in the twilight!

Sunkissed Blooms

Under the sun, the blooms do smile,
A ladybug prances, oh so versatile!
She spins around in a dazzling whirl,
Causing the petals to giggle and twirl.

The daisies chat with the sunniest rays,
Creating gossip in their flowery ways.
With every giggle, the garden roars,
As laughter dances through open doors.

Colorful Whimsy in the Wild

In the forest where colors play,
Little critters dance all day.
Bumblebees wear hats of fluff,
Singing tunes that are quite tough.

Squirrels juggle nuts with glee,
Laughing branches wave with spree.
A rainbow slipped on a bold dance,
Nature revels in her chance.

Petals in the Wind

Petals twirl like flying kites,
They spark joy in wild delights.
A curious frog leaps in surprise,
Chasing shadows, oh what a rise!

Butterflies don sparkling shoes,
Flitting about, refusing to snooze.
A giggle escapes from a tall tree,
Nature's laughter jumps with glee.

Celebration in the Canopy

Birds gathering for a grand feast,
Welcoming morning, primed for the least.
With berries mashed into a pie,
They're crafting smiles as they fly.

The sun peeks through, a cheeky grin,
Tickling leaves, it's where we begin.
All around, the jungle hums,
Its silly rhythm makes us drums.

Lushness in the Air

In the air, lush laughter blooms,
Whispers float in leafy rooms.
Gnomes in gardens swap tall tales,
While turtles share their silly wails.

Frogs don bow ties, ice cream sweet,
Merry meetings in drumming feet.
With every breath, joy's drawing near,
In this playful world, we cheer.

Blossoms in the Moonlight

Under the glow of the night,
Petals dance in delight,
Bumblebees buzzing with cheer,
Twirling round without any fear.

Laughter drips from each bloom,
As the garden finds its room,
A snail races with a napkin,
While the cat plots a fun fast action.

Moonbeams wink from the trees,
As a parody of bees,
The flowers giggle in hues,
Joining in playful muse.

So here we share a toast,
To the blossoms we love the most,
In laughter, we'll forever be,
In this floral jubilee.

Gardens of Whimsy

In a garden where giggles play,
Squirrels wear hats, come what may,
The daisies sing silly songs,
While the tulips dance along.

A gnome trips, oh what a sight,
Caught in a potato sack fight,
The petals join in a cheer,
Who knew gardens could be so dear?

With every flower that sways,
A blast from the past displays,
Old ladybugs tell funny tales,
Of daring and mischief, oh how it pales!

Such a zany floral spree,
Where each bloom runs wild and free,
Let's revel in this charming whim,
And lose ourselves on a joyful whim.

Petal Dreams

In dreams where petals take flight,
The sunflowers wear shades so bright,
While two frogs croon a duet,
Their voices sweet, no need to fret.

Chasing butterflies on loop,
A ladybug leads the troop,
Each bloom waits for a chance,
To join in the merry dance.

Dandelions puff and blow,
To join the laughter they know,
While hidden critters giggle near,
Cheering on each silly cheer.

So gather round, let's celebrate,
In this land of quirky fate,
With petal dreams and smiles wide,
In floral fun, we all collide.

Floral Fantasia

In a land of bright bouquet,
Where petals throw a cabaret,
The marigolds shake, prance, play,
While the roses join the fray.

A cactus breaks into a jig,
In a pair of boots so big,
The orchids strut with flair,
In this carnival of air.

Honeybees spin on a dime,
Create a buzz, oh so sublime,
While willow branches twirl about,
Laughing out loud, no single doubt.

So in this floral glee,
Let's laugh and dance, wild and free,
With petals floating, dreams in sway,
In our whimsical bouquet.

Mystical Petals in the Breeze

In gardens where the flowers dance,
Bees buzz around in a merry prance.
Colors clash like socks on a child,
Nature's own jokes, mischievously compiled.

Leaves giggle softly, the trees do grin,
As petals swirl round, a whimsical spin.
A butterfly lands with a comical flair,
Whispering secrets only flowers share.

Harmonies of Nature's Palette

The sun paints the sky with wild delight,
While squirrels steal snacks, quite a sight.
Amidst blooming laughter, the day takes flight,
Nature's refrain, a colorful bite.

The brook babbles jokes, stones giggle back,
Even the daisies join in the whack.
A marigold winks, a jester in bloom,
Telling the roses, "Make some more room!"

Fragrance of a Sunny Afternoon

On sunlit days, aromas arise,
Tickling noses, a sweet surprise.
Ants in a line, marching in tune,
Frolicsome footsteps under the noon.

The daffodils chuckle, oh what a smell!
Inviting the breeze to join in as well.
Laughter and scents drift lazily by,
As butterflies burst forth, oh my, oh my!

Echoes from the Blossom Trail

Along the path where blossoms hum,
Bees wear hats, oh what fun!
Petals scatter like confetti,
What a party, bright and yet petty!

Birds chirp tales from the leafy nook,
Clowns in the garden, take a good look!
Frogs leap about with a comical flair,
While flowers giggle, suspended in air.

Petals Under the Stars

Under the sky where petals twirl,
Dancing with joy, the blossoms unfurl.
Bees buzzing loud, they've joined the fun,
While nightingale sings 'til the day is done.

Frogs join the beat with a ribbiting cheer,
Their croaks make us laugh, oh dear, oh dear!
With a wink and a nod, the flowers sway,
In this wild garden, we laugh and play.

An Anthology of Color

Colors collide in a marvelous spree,
As flowers gossip like best friends, you see.
Orange and pink trade their silly jokes,
While purple rolls eyes at the antics of folks.

In this bloom-filled scene, there's no need to pout,
Just pluck a few petals and throw your doubts out.
The canvas of laughter paints hearts so bright,
With giggles and chuckles, we dance through the night.

In the Lap of Floral Luxury

Sitting on petals, like pillows of glee,
We sip on the nectar, wild and free.
A butterfly flutters, but trips on a vine,
While laughter erupts, like it's drinking fine wine.

The blooms are the guests, all dressed up in style,
Telling each other, 'You're fabulous, vile!'
With fragrance and giggles across the green space,
We toast to the flowers—a heavenly place.

Nature's Joyous Revelations

Nature's a jester with a floral bouquet,
Tickling our senses in a bright, funny way.
The daisies are snickering, it's not a charade,
While roses blush, feeling slightly betrayed.

In the tapestry woven of color and cheer,
The laughter of blooms is all that we hear.
A parade of petals that skedaddle and prance,
In this playful realm, we waltz in a dance.

Radiant Flush

In gardens where the blossoms thrive,
The bees all buzz, they dance and jive.
A flower's hat, all pink and bright,
Sways to the tune of pure delight.

Petals fall like confetti rain,
A polka dance, a floral gain.
With every twirl, the colors clash,
A memory made in a joyful splash.

The squirrels in suits take center stage,
Crying out, 'Yes, turn the page!'
With nature's jesters having fun,
Who knew the plants could be this one?

So grab your friends, let's sway along,
And join this merry, floral throng.
With laughter ringing through the day,
In this bright bloom, we'll shout hooray!

Nature's Joyful Conspiracy

Underneath the arching trees,
A winking flower whispers, 'Please!'
The daisies giggle, the tulips tease,
As nature plots its funny squeeze.

The birds all chirp in harmonies,
While ants in line book busking fees.
The butterflies take selfies, sly,
This floral scheme is quite the spy!

And when the sun begins to fall,
The shadows stretch and start to crawl.
A puppet show with vines unspooled,
Is this a plot? Oh, we're all fooled!

So here we are, in laughter's clutch,
With blossoms bold and petals such.
Join this riotous camaraderie,
For nature's schemes are quite the spree!

Echoes of Enchantment

In a field where colors clash,
A teasing flower starts to flash.
With violets singing tunes of glee,
Enchanting all who pause to see.

The wind plays tricks with every bloom,
As laughter fills the sunny room.
The roses gossip, the tulips reel,
In this bouquet, we share a meal.

A daffodil dipped in buttercup,
Says, 'Well, isn't life just sup?'
With petals twirling in a spin,
The echoes of joy, where to begin?

So come and join this floral fuss,
In petals soft, let's create a bus.
For here in smiles, we find our way,
In echoes of delight each day!

Harmony in the Petal Parade

In the meadow, the petals sway,
A carnival of colors at play.
With daisies marching, bold and loud,
They strut about, oh, so proud!

The sunbeams tickle every leaf,
While laughter flows, it's beyond belief.
The lilacs twirl, the poppies jump,
In this parade, there's no slump!

The butterflies in feathered flight,
Join the revelry, oh what a sight!
With every bloom a quirky jest,
This floral festive is simply the best!

Let's dance beneath this vibrant sky,
Where every flower gives a cry.
In harmony we wind and weave,
In this petal parade, we truly believe!

Vibrance in Every Leaf

In the garden, colors flare,
Flowers giggle, pollens share.
Bees in tuxedos, buzzing by,
Tickled petals wave hello, oh my!

Dancing buds with laughter sound,
Joyful hues whirl all around.
Nature's party on display,
Who knew green could dance this way?

A splash of pink, a dash of blue,
Singing squirrels, a funny crew.
Sunlight sprinkles, smiles arise,
Every leaf is in disguise!

Oh, come and join this floral jest,
Where colors prance and feel their best.
In this bouquet of charming glee,
Life's a blossom, wild and free!

Nature's Embrace of Color

A rainbow spun from roots so deep,
Flowers giggle, they can't sleep.
Frogs in hats start a parade,
While buzzing bees find their charade.

The daisies chat in whispered tones,
While trees break into silly moans.
Pansies laugh, they're such a tease,
Offering bribes of sweet-scented breeze.

Potatoes blush, feel out of place,
As tulips strut with perfect grace.
Worms declare it's time to dance,
In nature's ball, they take a chance!

So gather round this merry spree,
Where color clowns jig with glee.
Each bloom's a wink, a joyful cheer,
In this riot of flora we hold dear!

Hidden Meadows of Wonder

In secret fields where blooms will play,
Petals whisper the silliest way.
Butterflies paint in dizzying swirls,
With tiny hats and quirk-filled curls.

Rabbits hop in a hopscotch game,
While daisies giggle, never tame.
Bubbles float, the grass does sway,
Nature's laughter takes the day!

Gnomes offer jokes of the tallest sort,
To bees and bugs, a chuckling court.
Sunbeams shine, tickle and tease,
Hidden wonders that aim to please.

The meadow waits to tell its tale,
Of vibrant jokes in a floral gale.
Every petal knows how to jest,
In this secret, nature's best!

Festivity Among the Flowers

Flowers gather in wild parade,
Petal streamers, laughter, cascade.
The marigolds crack up in hues,
While lilies shake off morning dews.

Sunflowers raise their leafy arms,
Swaying proudly, showing charms.
Dahlias strut down a flowery lane,
In a comedic bloom display!

Waltzing weeds in a tangled dance,
Invite the bees for a sweet romance.
Poppy jokes float on the breeze,
While bugs break out in a chorus of wheeze!

Join the jubilee of every hue,
A flower fest made just for you.
In nature's net of laughter tight,
The petals sparkle, pure delight!

Flourishing Secrets Unearthed

In gardens where giggles bloom,
Flowers plot in their perfume.
Petals whisper tales of cheer,
Secrets shared when no one's near.

The bees wear tiny party hats,
Dancing 'round with fancy chats.
Gardener trips, his spade goes flying,
"Patch up that hole," we hear him crying.

Insects jest beneath the sun,
Ladybugs call it all in fun.
"More color!" shout the blooms with glee,
Paint the world, oh let it be!

With petals tangled in a dance,
Nature laughs, given the chance.
Unruly joy spills everywhere,
A floral jest, beyond compare.

Conversations with Color

A violet beckons, "What's your hue?"
A sunflower grins and says, "Who knew?"
Pinks are chirping, reds are loud,
In this garden, joy's avowed.

"Lavender gossip," says the sage,
"Let's turn this patch into a stage!"
Orange zinnias crack a joke,
While daisies nod, their laughter stoked.

Butterflies engaged in debate,
"Who's prettier? Oh, isn't it great?"
With every flap, the colors sway,
In this chatter, bright and gay.

Budding blooms in comic mood,
Jests exchanged like seeds of food.
The riot of shades, a fanciful sight,
In nature's circus, everything's bright.

Tidal Waves of Floral Joy

Waves of petals crash like the sea,
Laughter stirs, wild and free.
Daffodils surf on the breeze,
While tulips squeal, "Oh, do as you please!"

A daisy waves to a laughing friend,
"In flower power, there's no end!"
Bouquet brawls and pollen fights,
Under soft, dancing daylight nights.

In marigold swims, they splash about,
Joyous chirps and merry shout.
A riotous bloom, (who's counting the cost?)
In this floral sea, none are lost.

Nature's waves, rolling with mirth,
Declare that laughter's the best on Earth.
So dip your petals, join the cheer,
In this floral hilarity, far and near.

The Colorful Echo of Nature

Echoes burst from every bloom,
Colors chime like laughter's tune.
Petals giggle in the light,
Nature's chorus, pure delight.

"There's a bluebird in that rose!"
"Can he sing?" a garden knows.
Foliage chimes in with a tease,
"Now that's a sight that aims to please!"

A patch of green pops out to play,
"Frolic here, the whole day!"
Mirthful hues compete for eyes,
"Who's the brightest?" Nature sighs.

Every shade has stories spun,
Together bursting, just for fun.
With laughter loud and colors bold,
Nature's echo never grows old.

Embrace of the Blooming World

In the garden, flowers laugh,
A daisy in a top hat strikes a pose.
Tulips tell jokes to the daffodils,
While bees buzz along in fancy clothes.

Petals dance and spin with glee,
Each bud a comedian in its own right.
A squirrel joins in the wacky scene,
Chasing shadows in the warm sunlight.

Nature's circus, what a sight,
With the breeze as our cheering crowd.
Blossoms sway with joyous delight,
Celebrating life, oh so loud!

Let's sip nectar, have a spree,
As laughter blooms amidst the green.
A bright bouquet, wild and free,
In this silly, sunny scene!

The Language of Blossoms

Petals whisper secrets soft,
In vibrant hues, they share their dreams.
A rose tells tales from far aloft,
While tulips giggle in silly themes.

Laughter ripples through the leaves,
As nature's parrot squawks on cue.
Forget-me-nots pull up their sleeves,
Saying, "Don't forget us, too!"

Marigolds make puns of gold,
And sunflowers break into a dance.
Their banter, a joy to behold,
As they plot a whimsical romance.

In this bloom bazaar, we spread cheer,
With every fragrance, love will grow.
Oh silly blooms, how sweet you appear,
In this garden's radiant glow!

Serenade of the Garden Paths

Down the paths of petals bright,
Silly bumbles hum a tune.
Floral notes take flight at night,
Underneath the silly moon.

Butterflies waltz, they glide and sway,
Dancing with the drifty breeze.
Every bloom has something to say,
A secret whispered with such ease.

Dandelions laugh at their own fluff,
They fly away, no care in sight.
Rosy cheeks, a garden of stuff,
Filling hearts with pure delight.

Through the paths where laughter flows,
With sprinkle of petals, joy will reign.
Nature's song, everyone knows,
In this garden, fun is the gain!

Captured Moments in Full Bloom

Snap a pic of the giggling greens,
As blossoms pose like stars on stage.
A lilac's wink on the scene,
While marigolds turn every page.

Bumblebees in their buzzing suits,
Mimic models with every flight.
The flowers curtsy in their roots,
In this moment, pure delight.

Chasing wild dreams in every hue,
The snapdragons play peek-a-boo.
Carnival colors shining through,
A vibrant show just for me and you.

So let's capture this bloom-filled jest,
A funny world in shades so bright.
In every petal lies a quest,
To find the joy, our hearts ignite!

A Burst of Floral Laughter

In a garden bright and merry,
Petals dance like kids so merry.
Bees buzz about with silly glee,
Chasing dreams as wild as can be.

Floral hats upon their heads,
They prance around like singing threads.
Each bloom a joke, a laugh to share,
Nature's jesters without a care.

Sunshine beams a cheerful grin,
While dandelions leap in.
With every gust, they play and swirl,
A comical floral world.

So join the fun, don't be late,
Let flowers bloom and laughter sate.
In this garden, joy turns bright,
Where laughter blooms from day to night.

The Blooming Celebration

Colors burst as springtime rises,
With laughter in the air, disguises.
Every bloom a silly face,
Gathered here in merry grace.

Petals flit like feathered dancers,
Wobbling here, they take their chances.
Sunbeams tease, the shadows play,
Silly games in bright display.

Each flower takes its turn to twirl,
In the wind, they laugh and whirl.
A sweet aroma fills the scene,
Like a party, bright and keen.

Who knew nature had a plan,
To throw a bash just for us fans?
Come, sit down, don't miss the thrill,
In this bloom-filled laughter spill.

Arboreal Harmony

Trees join in, a leafy cheer,
Roots are tapping, sound so clear.
Branches sway in rhythmic song,
While blossoms burst, can't go wrong.

Squirrels giggle, hiding nuts,
While flower jokes fill their guts.
Nature laughs from root to crown,
This leafy carnival goes down.

Flutter by, a butterfly,
With painted wings, oh my, oh my!
It tickles blooms, they giggle loud,
Creating quite a woodland crowd.

So join the dance, unleash your soul,
In this harmony, we're all whole.
With laughter ringing through the trees,
Find your joy in nature's breeze.

Colors Colliding in Nature's Canopy

Underneath the boughs so wide,
Colors clash, they coincide.
Pink and yellow, red and blue,
A wild party blooms anew.

Flowers bounce and make a tease,
Bees are buzzing, swinging with ease.
Nature's palette bursts with cheer,
All things silly gather here.

Little critters join the fun,
Chasing shadows, on the run.
Many hues, a joyous sight,
In this riot of pure delight.

So laugh with blooms, spin and sway,
Celebrate this merry day.
Where every color finds its place,
In this whimsical, joyous space.

Swaying Spirits of the Wildflower

In the garden, flowers dance,
Swaying to a breezy romance.
Petals twirl in silly glee,
Buzzing bees join the spree.

Laughter blooms with every hue,
Bright yellows, pinks, and lavender too.
A butterfly slips on a flower's face,
Spinning round in a polka race.

The bunnies hop with joyous cheer,
Wearing dandelions like a crown of beer.
With every laugh, the colors glow,
Nature's party, the greatest show!

So come along, find your place,
Join the fragrance, feel the grace.
In this wildflower, funny fiesta,
Life's a giggle, what a siesta!

A Celebration of Spring's Colors

Spring comes in with a confetti burst,
Colors flying, oh what a thirst!
Yellow tulips wear silly hats,
While dancing squirrels do acrobats.

Pink daisies gossip with the grass,
Meeting on, they all amass.
"Did you hear the news?" they tease,
"Frogs are planning a ball with bees!"

Crickets chirp in harmony,
Jokes abound, a comedy!
Purple violets try to sing,
But lost their notes in the swing.

With laughter bright, the flowers play,
In this springtime, come what may.
Join the fun, don't be shy,
A riot of color beneath the sky!

When Blooms Take the Stage

On the stage of nature's glee,
Blooms prance forth theatrically.
Sunflowers bow, tulips swoon,
A daisy's flop makes us croon.

"Look at me!" a rose declares,
Winking clouds offer dainty flares.
The lilacs chuckle, wearing capes,
As pansies make the funniest shapes.

Bees take tickets, buzzing loud,
While ladybugs cheer for the crowd.
Each flower tries a solo dance,
As petals spin in a wild trance.

Curtains close on a blooming sight,
Amidst the laughter and delight.
Nature's show, don't miss the cue,
This floral comedy's just for you!

Tapestry of Nature's Joy

In the meadow, colors weave,
A tapestry that won't deceive.
From red to blue, the shades combine,
Where flowers giggle, all align.

A jester bee trips on a stem,
Spilling nectar in a gem.
Sunlight dances on a patch,
Nature's laughter in the batch.

Petunias gossip with a grin,
Sharing secrets on the wind.
Seedlings play hide and seek,
While grasses tickle with a peek.

So join the fun, release your frown,
In this tapestry, let's clown around.
With nature's humor, life employs,
A joyous burst in every voice!

Nectar of the Garden's Heart

In the garden where blooms jest,
Bumblebees dance, feeling blessed.
With petals wide, they take a sip,
On nectar sweet, they take a trip.

A rabbit hops, wearing a hat,
Sipping tea where flowers spat.
The daisies giggle, the roses sway,
In this riot of colors, they play all day.

Giggling frogs join the merry throng,
Singing loud their silly song.
Butterflies pirouette on air,
In this humorous garden affair.

When night falls, the fireflies gleam,
In the moonlight, they weave a dream.
The laughter echoes, soft and bright,
In nature's joy, pure delight.

Spirited Petal Pilgrimage

A band of blooms set out one morn,
To search for laughter, unadorned.
With every step, sprigs play peek,
In the breeze, they start to squeak.

The tulips trumpet silly tunes,
While violets dance under the moons.
Chasing shadows, they skip and hop,
As petals twirl, they never stop.

Sunflowers giggle, doing their dance,
In this botanical, bright romance.
The lilies laugh in vibrant jest,
In petals' play, we find our zest.

The journey swirls, a vivid ride,
Where whimsy waits, we laugh and glide.
Through gardens lush, in hearty cheers,
The blooms unite, erasing fears.

Beneath the Cascading Blooms

Under blossoms that sway and spin,
A squirrel sneaks, grinning with a grin.
With acorns, he juggles, a funny sight,
While petals rain down, a pure delight.

A parade of bees buzzes with glee,
As the flower crowd joins in the spree.
The blooms wear hats, a mismatched view,
In this carnival, all colors brew.

Chirping birds burst into song,
In the tangled weeds, they all belong.
A toad in a tie croaks with flair,
Beneath the blooms, laughter fills the air.

As shadows stretch, they wink and play,
In the twilight glow, fun's here to stay.
Nature chuckles in playful fun,
Under cascading blooms, we run.

The Blossom's Gentle Lullaby

At dusk, when petals start to close,
The garden hums in soft repose.
A ladybug strums a tiny tune,
While sleepy bees drift 'neath the moon.

The roses whisper secrets dear,
While tulips giggle, loud and clear.
Fireflies blink in a winking jest,
In this serene, whimsical nest.

Dandelions dance, bowing low,
In the night breeze, they steal the show.
Moths flutter by, with gentle grace,
In this tender, floral embrace.

Softly now, the garden sighs,
As dreams of blooms fill the skies.
In nature's cradle, humor flows,
With laughter where the blossom grows.

The Garden's Serenade

In the garden, a dance takes flight,
Bumblebees buzzing, what a sight!
Petals prance under sunlit beams,
Wiggling weeds join in our dreams.

Daffodils giggle, tulips tease,
Chasing shadows, waving with ease.
A gopher bursts from his cozy nook,
Shocked by a curious, watching crook.

Butterflies flutter, socks askew,
Wearing styles we never knew.
The sunflowers grin, a comical show,
As wind whispers secrets, thought you'd know!

In this quirky patch, joy's the key,
Where laughter blooms like herbs in spree.
Join the frolic, plant your cheer,
Amidst the chaos, fun is near!

Nature's Swaying Tapestry

Twisted vines make a fine display,
Hanging hats in a merry array.
A squirrel squawks, oh what a jest,
Chasing his tail, he thinks he's the best!

Dancing daisies dip and dive,
While clumsy ants try to arrive.
The soil laughs with each soft thud,
As blooms reveal their colorful bud.

Bumblebees wear suits of gold,
Telling tales that never get old.
The maidenhair fern waves its fronds,
Encouraging friends to get beyond!

Petunias play their hidden game,
While daisies complain of the fame.
Nature's fabric, stitched with glee,
A patchwork of fun, you see!

Emerald Canopy Dreams

Under the boughs where the green leaves hide,
A frog croaks loudly—a humorous guide.
With every leap and hearty squawk,
He claims the trail like a peacock!

The ferns shuffle, trying to impress,
As sunlight glimmers, a hilarious mess.
In hidden corners, misfits convene,
Whispering gossip, a playful scene!

The ladybugs march, all in a line,
Suddenly slip on a grapevine!
In this emerald dream, laughter flows,
With every petal, mischief grows!

A canopy of green, a merry sight,
Where whimsy dances and hearts take flight.
Join the shenanigans, don't you wait,
In this leafy haven, we celebrate!

Echoes of the Flowering Path

On the path where blossoms twirl,
A giggling butterfly gives a whirl.
Petals scatter, a playful breeze,
Time for a dance, if you please!

Sunshine tickles, shadows play,
Chasing beetles down the way.
Each flower tells a joke or two,
While daisies nod, agreeing too!

A parakeet sings a funny tune,
While daisies sway beneath the moon.
In harmony, the insects sigh,
With laughter lifting spirits high!

Follow the echoes, hear the cheer,
In this floral realm where joy is clear.
So take a step, and feel the laugh,
In nature's bloom, we'll have a blast!

Vibrant Rhapsody of Nature

In gardens bright, the flowers dance,
They twirl and leap with carefree chance.
Petals giggle, colors sing,
Nature's joy, a lively fling.

Bumblebees wear tiny hats,
They sip on nectar, chitchat with bats.
Sunshine sprinkles all around,
Frolics in the floral ground.

The daisies wear their merry crowns,
While tulips sway in playful gowns.
Laughter blooms on every bough,
Come join the fun, don't miss it now!

A breeze whispers silly things,
As butterflies burst forth on wings.
Oh, what a sight, what a sound,
In this realm, joy is profound!

Ode to the Floral Spirits

Oh, little blooms, such cheeky cheer,
With every petal, you spread good cheer.
In gardens wide, you prance around,
A floral circus, joy unbound.

The violets play hide and seek,
While daisies giggle, oh so meek.
Pansies wink with painted eyes,
As butterflies hold grand disguise.

Petunias tell the funniest jokes,
While lily pads host stealthy folks.
The sun, a jester, shines so bright,
In nature's play, all is delight.

With twinkling stars, the night arrives,
And all the blooms share silly dives.
In this tapestry of glee,
The floral spirits dance with thee!

The Joyful Chorus of Spring

Awake, awake! The flowers cry,
As spring arrives with a winked eye.
With polka dots and stripes so grand,
They form a band across the land.

The tulips strut in fancy shoes,
While daisies sing the silliest blues.
In the greenhouse, giggles thrum,
With every seed, a punchline's hum.

The roses have a ticklish stem,
Their fragrance calls, 'Come dance with them!'
Jolly gardens, full of life,
In nature's jest, there's no more strife.

So join the crowd, don't stay away,
In bloomtime cheer, we laugh and play.
The chorus swells, so bright, so bold,
In spring's embrace, the joy unfolds!

Blossoming Whimsy in the Air

Flowers laugh as the breeze flits by,
They tickle sunbeams, oh my, oh my!
Petals tumble, bright colors collide,
A whimsy whirlwind, come take a ride.

The lilies wear their shades so cool,
While daisies form a merry school.
In every hue, they bloom and tease,
Nature's fun in the gentle breeze.

With glee, the sun draws smiles in gold,
And shadows stretch, a sight to behold.
Hydrangeas blush with a playful grin,
As springtime antics all begin.

So frolic on through this floral maze,
In blooming laughter, let's soak up rays.
The world of whimsy, so full of flair,
A joyful feast beyond compare!

Whimsy Under the Canopy

Underneath the leafy boughs,
A dance begins with silly sows.
Bumbles buzz, and twirls they make,
In laughter lost, we shake and quake.

The squirrels don their tiny hats,
And join the fun with chitter-chat.
Frogs leap high, with graceful flair,
In nature's jest, we giggle, stare.

The sun peeks through, a bright confetti,
As blooms surround, oh what a jetty!
Colors splash in joyous cheer,
Under the trees, we shed a tear.

Come find your jolly hiding spot,
Where every joke is tied in knots.
The fun unfolds beneath the sky,
In crazy hues, we fly, we fly!

An Ode to Brightness

Oh hues so bright, like laughter's sound,
In every petal joy is found.
The bees wear shades, and dance around,
Creating songs that bust the ground.

Such vivid pinks, and yellows too,
Like giggles whispered out of view.
A cheerful breeze will play the flute,
In nature's band, what a hoot!

With every puff, the clouds conspire,
To tickle blooms, and spark desire.
As butterflies with mischief caper,
Their bright confetti, nature's paper.

So raise a toast, with silly grace,
To every smile, to every face.
In this bright world where laughter flows,
Let's join the fun, as friendship grows!

Rhythms of Nature's Palette

Nature's brush, it sips with glee,
Painting smiles on every tree.
A striped skunk, with gusto flaunts,
His whimsical waltz, a stinky jaunt.

The flowers sway to tunes unheard,
As chirps and bubbles are transferred.
A multitasking tortoise strums,
And joins the fun, while everyone hums.

Ribbons of color spin and twirl,
While ladybugs in circles whirl.
With laughter echoing, it's clear,
The palette plays upon our cheer.

Let's waddle forth, no need to hide,
In nature's dance, we'll side by side.
With every beat, our spirits lift,
In this grand show, the greatest gift!

The Secret Life of Blossoms

The blossoms giggle, pink and spry,
Gossiping as the breezes sigh.
They tie their leaves in silly knots,
As blossoms plan their funny plots.

A bee with googly eyes zooms about,
Wearing a tiny, striped scout route.
He fumbles flowers, oh what a pun!
In the garden's jest, we all have fun.

Secret lives beneath the sun,
Where petals peek and stamen run.
In every hue, a chuckle's born,
Nature's jest, like a crown adorned.

So wander near where tickles bloom,
And let them lift away your gloom.
In laughter's breath, we all convene,
Among the colors, joy is seen!

Beyond the Bloom

In a garden where colors dance,
Petals giggle as they prance,
Buzzing bees in silly flight,
Turn the day into pure delight.

Bumblebees wearing tiny hats,
Chasing butterflies and chatty rats,
Here comes a snail, moving quite slow,
Sipping dew in the morning glow.

Rabbits hop, wearing shoes so bright,
Making mischief from day till night,
Flowers burst in laughter loud,
Nature's jesters, proud and bowed.

Underneath the trees they play,
Juggling petals in a ballet,
As sunbeams join the merry spree,
It's a world of joy, wild and free.

Joyful Fragrance in the Air

A whiff of giggles drifts around,
As blooms and laughs abound,
Dancing leaves on a wavy breeze,
Rustle jokes from the playful trees.

Squirrels wear their finest ties,
Trading secrets, oh what a surprise!
With twirling vines as their dance floor,
Who could ask for anything more?

The dew drops, like jesters, play,
On every petal, all night and day,
In this garden, joy flows free,
Nature's laughter, a symphony.

A riot of colors, bright and bold,
Each flower, a tale waiting to be told,
With scents that sparkle and tickle your nose,
Creating smiles wherever it goes.

Dreaming in Pastels

Pastel petals, soft and sweet,
Whispering tales as they meet,
Sunshine giggles in every hue,
Tickling noses, just like dew.

A frog in a tutu croaks a song,
While clouds above dance along,
Painting rainbows with a splash,
As daisies giggle in a dash.

In this dreamscape, laughter flows,
With each breeze, a new joke grows,
The butterflies in their attire,
Join the fun, won't soon retire.

Every petal has a part,
In this garden of joyful art,
With humor spun from nature's loom,
Creating a vibrant, blissful bloom.

Lush Landscapes of Bliss

Lush landscapes with joy to share,
Blooming giggles fill the air,
Grinning flowers, what a scene,
Frolicking as if in a dream.

Ducks in bow ties quack in tune,
Beneath the laughter of the moon,
With fireflies painting with their light,
Turning shadows into delight.

The grass tickles each toe that walks,
As flowers gather for silly talks,
In every corner, fun does sprout,
Making sure no one's left out.

In this haven, where smiles collide,
Nature's humor is our guide,
So let us dance 'neath skies so wide,
In blooming joy, we take our stride.

Hidden Gardens of Delight

In the garden, blooms collide,
Bees in costumes, quite the sight.
Dancing petals, side by side,
Who knew flowers could take flight?

With giggles and a puff of air,
A dandelion takes a bow.
Tulips wear a silly stare,
As squirrels dance and say, "Wow!"

Behind the leaves, a party brews,
A butterfly spills juice with glee.
Everyone's got silly shoes,
Even the ants, oh look and see!

In hidden corners, joy does sprout,
A snail slips by, all full of cheer.
This garden's what it's all about,
With hearty laughter buzzing near.

Blossoms Burst into Song

Petals strum on leafy strings,
Glorious notes dance in the breeze.
A daffodil off-key sings,
While lilies sway with perfect ease.

A chorus of a hues brigade,
Flowering friends in funny hats.
Dancing up, they won't be weighed,
Giggling lightly at the bats.

Hummingbirds tap in a beat,
Strawberries twirl with joyous flair.
Nature's tune, a treat to greet,
As grasshoppers leap without care.

In this garden of pure delight,
Laughter echoes, blooms all day.
Funny voices take to flight,
Amidst the flowers, dance, and play.

A Tapestry of Floral Dreams

Petals stitched in vibrant hues,
The raccoons wear a flower crown.
While bees swap their buzzing blues,
A ladybug wants to jump down.

Each bloom shares a tale to tell,
As wind plays their funny song.
Peonies chuckle, all is swell,
And daisies dance the whole night long.

In this vivid patchwork spree,
A sunflower steals the spotlight.
Showing off its quirky glee,
A shy bud jumps, "Oh, what a sight!"

Together they weave laughter bright,
In gardens where dreams take to flight.
This tapestry, a funny scene,
Where flowers laugh, row by row, keen.

The Blooming Chronicles

In stories spun from roots and leaves,
Each petal has its own intrigue.
A cactus jokes with swaying eaves,
As violets wiggle with fatigue.

The daises chuckle side by side,
As merry as a morn can be.
Jasmine's tales, a knotted ride,
Tickling the grass with glee, you see.

The foliage whispers secrets sweet,
A gossip mound of green delight.
With every turn, new friends they meet,
Frolicking till they dance at night.

So come and join this floral tale,
Where blooms unite and laughter flies.
With every twist and funny trail,
In every petal, joy complies.

Sunlit Paths Through Petal Rain

In a garden where blooms play,
Bumblebees dance, oh what a day!
Petals tumble from trees above,
Nature's confetti, a gift of love.

The sun winks down, what a scene,
Squirrels plotting in shades of green.
They steal the spotlight, a bold reprise,
While flowers giggle under bright blue skies.

Frogs wear crowns of leafy flair,
They croak and ribbit without a care.
The air is thick with laughter sweet,
As daisies twirl in a cheerful beat.

So grab your friends, don't be late,
Join in the fun, let's celebrate!
For in this patch of mirth and cheer,
We'll spread our joy, it's quite clear!

The Awakening of Floral Dreams

As night gives way to daylight play,
Blossoms yawn, it's time to sway.
Bees don their hats, with elegant flair,
Busy little critters, whisking through air.

A dandelion tells a silly joke,
The petals giggle, oh what a poke!
Tulips strut in their vibrant dress,
Cracking up, they're quite the mess.

Clouds shape-shift into puffy sheep,
As flowers awaken from their sleep.
The colors burst, a palette so bright,
Making flowers dance with sheer delight.

So come and join this comical sight,
Where nature smiles with pure delight.
Let laughter bloom in fragrant streams,
In this wacky world of floral dreams.

A Festival Beneath the Canopy

Gather round, let's throw a bash,
Under the trees, we'll make a splash.
Ferns in skirts, twirling so fast,
Making merry with a giggle blast.

The sun peeks in with a mischievous eye,
As butterflies flutter, oh me, oh my!
They bring the cake, a sweet delight,
Celebrating life, what a funny sight!

Ants march in, a parade on the ground,
With tiny drums, they'll make a sound.
The breeze carries laughter here and there,
Nature's jesters, spreading cheer in the air.

So raise a toast to this woodland feast,
Where humor blooms, and joy won't cease.
Under the canopy, let's laugh and play,
In this festival of flora, we'll stay!

Jubilant Colors of the Wild

In the wild where colors clash,
Flowers burst like a cheeky splash.
Reds and yellows, oh what a sight,
Painting the world with pure delight.

Grasshoppers dance in crazy lines,
While daisies gossip with playful pines.
Laughing buds nod as they greet,
This vibrant chaos, a happy treat.

The wind joins in, a raucous cheer,
Whispering secrets for all to hear.
Cacti chuckle, their spines hold tight,
Sharing their stories in laughter's light.

So take a step into this vivid blend,
Let your spirit rise, let your heart mend.
With jubilant colors, we joyfully tread,
In this wild garden, where humor's spread!

Colorful Confetti of the Earth

In the garden, colors clash,
Petals dancing, making a splash.
Bees wear tiny party hats,
While ants perform their acrobat acts.

Squirrels in a conga line,
Stealing snacks, oh so divine.
Budding blooms just have to shake,
They giggle loud, for goodness' sake!

Sunlight spills like bright confetti,
While the grass plays soft and petty.
Nature's laughter fills the air,
As flowers prance without a care.

With each bloom, the joy complies,
A carnival beneath the skies.
Let's join the fun, no need to think,
For life's a bash, just grab a drink!

Petal-Soft Journeys Through Time

Time travels on petal wings,
Whispers of joy, and laughter springs.
Flowers dressed for every dance,
Taking us on a silly chance.

Oh, the petals tell their tales,
Of silly birds and buttered snails.
A snail in shades, no need to rush,
While daisies giggle in a hush.

Bouncing blooms that love to roam,
Turning gardens into foam.
Petal parties by the brook,
Join them now, just take a look!

Every color, every hue,
In this world, there's fun for you.
Life can be a funny climb,
With petals soft, let's freeze the time!

Blooming Whispers

In the meadow, secrets bloom,
Petals whisper, chase away gloom.
The tulips giggle, "What a sight!"
While lilacs laugh, oh what a night!

Crickets cracking jokes, oh dear,
As butterflies simply cheer.
Rabbits stumble, trip, and dive,
Putting on a show, alive!

The daisies tease with each soft sway,
While bumblebees hum along the way.
Nature's jesters play their part,
With every bloom, they steal the heart.

So listen close, and you may find,
The blooms are witty and quite kind.
A humor dance upon the breeze,
Where laughter echoes through the trees!

Petals in the Breeze

Petals flutter, take a chance,
Catch the breeze and start to dance.
A comical swirl, a jolly twist,
Nature's pranks you can't resist.

Butterfly waits with a sly grin,
As flowers giggle, let the fun begin!
Twirling colors, vibrant and bright,
Stirring giggles into the night.

In the field of whimsy, prance about,
With petals flying, there's no doubt.
Grasshoppers leap with wild delight,
Creating joy from morning to night.

So embrace the whimsy, feel the cheer,
With petals dancing, nothing to fear.
Together we'll laugh, we'll sing, we'll play,
In this joyful world where petals sway.

Blooming Tales Unfold

In the garden, flowers sway,
With petals dancing in delight.
Bees are buzzing all around,
While ants put on a funny fight.

A hedgehog sports a flower crown,
Claiming he's the garden king.
The rabbits hop and tumble down,
While laughing birds begin to sing.

The sun is shining on the scene,
With colors bright and laughter loud.
A chipmunk tries to act so smooth,
But trips and falls—oh how he's proud!

As twilight drapes its dusky veil,
The blooms wink in the fading light.
With petals wide, they share the tale,
Of how they danced all day and night.

Floral Reverie

A daisy made a silly face,
With petals poking out askew.
The roses giggle, full of grace,
As daisies plot their next big coup.

Jasmine whispers secret dreams,
While violets spin in joyful glee.
An overly proud tulip beams,
Flaunting what it claims to be.

Buzzing bees try humor too,
As pollen cakes make them feel bold.
A dance-off in the sunlit dew,
Where flowers flaunt their colors gold!

In shadows cast by fragrant blooms,
The night unveils a starry waltz.
With laughter echoing through the gloom,
The blooms unite without a halt.

Unfurling the Garden's Heart

Amongst the petals, pranks abound,
With butterflies that tease and sway.
The sunflowers all turn around,
To join a game of hide and play.

A sneaky snail is on the run,
With clever tricks to fool the crew.
While clovers cheer, they have their fun,
As silly antics ensue anew.

The lilacs wear their fanciest hues,
While daisies tumble down the slope.
Each blossom crafts its own funny blues,
In gardens where all creatures cope.

The twilight glimmers soft and sweet,
As shadows dance with petals light.
In joy, the blossoms find their beat,
Spreading laughter through the night.

Twilight Blossoms

As evening falls, the scene is set,
With blooms that wink and tease a bit.
A silly rose jumps up and bets,
That no one can resist its wit.

The poppies giggle in a row,
Playing tag with fireflies bright.
Daisies sway in soft moon glow,
While tulips twirl with pure delight.

A bunny hops right through the scene,
With petals tangled in its fur.
The garden's filled with laughter keen,
As flowers join in a night blur.

When stars light up the floral space,
Each blossom sings a silly tune.
Under the watch of the moon's face,
In this realm, fun blooms always swoon.

A Dance of Colors

In the garden, colors collide,
Petals twirl, they won't abide.
A purple giggle, a pinky cheer,
Nature's disco, come dance here!

Bees in bow ties, buzzing along,
Wearing their stripes, they join the throng.
Butterflies flit in a silly parade,
Flowers chuckle, unafraid!

Daisies dip in the evening light,
Jiving with laughter, what a sight!
Every bloom brings a joke or two,
Nature's punchline, bright and true!

So grab a friend, come take a chance,
Join the blooms in a silly dance.
Under the sky, so vast and wide,
Laughter blooms, let it be your guide.

Secrets of the Mountain Bloom

High in the hills, what secrets lie?
A flower whispers, stars in the sky.
Jokes in petals, laughter confined,
Ticklish leaves, aren't nature's designs?

A fox in glasses, reads out a joke,
While raccoons gather around the oak.
"Why did the flower refuse to grow?
It couldn't find its roots, just so you know!"

Pine trees giggle in gentle sways,
As wee ones play in colorful displays.
Each bloom tells tales of mishaps grand,
In this secret, funny land!

Under the stars, every giggle's free,
The mountain full of joy and glee.
So come and listen, don't miss the show,
To the whispers of blooms in the moon's soft glow.

Symphony of Blossoms

In the orchestra of petals, what a sound!
A melodious giggle, joy all around.
Conductor bee, in stripes of gold,
Leading the blooms with stories bold!

Trumpets of tulips, laughter on cue,
Shouting sweet tunes, as skies turn blue.
Cactus joins in with a prickly grin,
Singing along to the swell within.

Lily pads dance on the puddle's face,
In harmony, they spin with grace.
A comedy show beneath the trees,
Where nature chuckles on a gentle breeze!

So let the petals play, let the blossoms sing,
Join the chorus, let laughter spring.
Life's a grand symphony, let's take a chance,
In this garden of joy, come and dance!

Vibrant Hues in Twilight

Twilight hues, a painter's delight,
Colors collide in soft fading light.
A sunset giggles, tints the sky,
Whispering secrets as day waves goodbye.

The primroses giggle at dusk's soft cheer,
While crickets chuckle, their songs sincere.
Fireflies blink their lights like stars,
Vying for laughter, all the way from afar!

Dandelions puff their fluffy heads,
Spreading wishes, as laughter spreads.
"Why did the rose wear shades at night?
It heard the stars were looking quite bright!"

So sip the colors, as evening grows,
Every bloom blooms, where silliness flows.
In the twilight's arms, let joy take flight,
In vibrant hues, all feels just right!

Enchanted Grove of Pink Delight

In a grove where giggles bloom,
Flowers chat and share their room.
A bee swings high, a butterfly flops,
Nature's dance, it never stops.

Petals wearing tiny hats,
Telling jokes like clever cats.
A squirrel stumbles on a vine,
"I swear I'm sober, I'm just fine!"

Sunshine spills, it spills with glee,
Tickling leaves on every tree.
Mice with trumpets, singing loud,
Join the merriment, feeling proud.

With each bloom, the laughter grows,
As frolicking winds blow through the rose.
The day ends with a giggly sigh,
In the grove, where fun will never die.

A Symphony of Blooms at Dusk

As dusk creeps in, the sky turns red,
Flowers play tunes, merry and spread.
A crocus strums its golden strings,
While daisies dance and trip on wings.

A poppy plays the tuba loud,
Making the nearby frogs feel proud.
Hummingbirds join the wild parade,
Zooming through petals, their antics made.

Blossoms giggle with fragrant zest,
While the moon prepares for its big jest.
Bees do the tango, buzzing in cheer,
As the night unfolds, the laughter's clear.

Nature's orchestra, wildly free,
Conducted by a busy bumblebee.
In the dusk, where blooms unite,
Their funny symphony takes flight.

The Secret Garden's Laughter

In a garden where secrets play,
Plants gossip about the day.
A rose slaps a thistle with glee,
"Oh, you thorny, can't you see?"

The daisies tease the sleepy ferns,
While a wise old snail slowly turns.
"Who's wearing pink? Oh, what a sight!"
"Not me," says grass, "I'm dressed in light!"

Charming seeds share silly tales,
Of brave adventures on flower trails.
A sunflower winks at passing bees,
"Careful, friends, don't land with ease!"

With every giggle, the petals glow,
In a secret nook where laughter flows.
All creatures join in playful cheer,
In the garden where fun's sincere.

Floral Fantasia in the Meadow

In the meadow where colors burst,
Flowers flirt, oh how they thirst!
A tulip spins in a wild whirl,
While daisies laugh and twirl and twirl.

A pink petal throws a dance fit,
"Come on, join in! Don't just sit!"
Butterflies flutter on playful prance,
Reveling in this floral chance.

Each blossom wears a jolly face,
And plays games in a vibrant space.
Grassy jokes fly with gentle breeze,
While ants join in, happy as bees.

Sunset paints their merry show,
In the meadow, where spirits glow.
With every petal, joy's a theme,
In the floral dream, they all beam.

Essence of Spring's Embrace

In the garden, blooms collide,
Petals giggle, side by side.
Bees in tutus dance and hum,
Nature's party, oh so fun!

Butterflies in crazy flight,
Wearing colors, oh so bright.
Daisies tease and poke their heads,
While daisies plot in flower beds!

Laughter echoes, soft and sweet,
As blooms tap dance with two left feet.
Spring's embrace, a wild delight,
A floral festival in sight!

So raise a glass, or sip some tea,
To petals prancing with such glee.
In this bloom-filled, fragrant cheer,
Join the fun, the springtime's here!

Sylvan Splendor Unveiled

In the woods, the ferns twist and twirl,
While squirrels in capes start to whirl.
Mushrooms giggle, stand in line,
Their polka dots, oh how they shine!

The trees play tag with the sunny rays,
While shadows dance in quirky ways.
A raccoon juggles acorns with flair,
And owls wink, pretending to care!

Frogs croak jokes on lily pads,
As each one tries to play the fads.
With splashes and hops, they claim their space,
Nature's laughter warms the place!

So wander forth through woods so grand,
Enjoy the fun, join the band.
Life's a show, with smiles and glee,
Sylvan wonders, come and see!

Chasing Shadows of Sunshine

Underneath the sun's warm gaze,
Flowers compete in funny ways.
Some twist left, while others slide,
Chasing shadows with pure pride!

A petal pirate steals the scene,
With an eye patch and a grin so mean.
Sunflowers serenade the crowd,
As daisies giggle, sweet and loud!

Caterpillars wear their hats,
As ladybugs host silly chats.
Butterflies teasing in a dance,
Trying to give the sun a chance!

So skip along, don't mind the fuss,
Join the chase; it's a great plus.
In fields of joy, let laughter blend,
Chasing shadows until day's end!

The Petal's Journey Home

Once a bud, with dreams so bright,
Wandering on a starry night.
Through rain puddles and muddy trails,
With laughter that never fails!

Dancing winds whisper a tune,
As petals sway beneath the moon.
A bumblebee's aerial chat,
Sends giggles where the wild things sat!

In search of soil, rich and warm,
To dodge the storm, to chase the norm.
With each gust, a twirl and spin,
The journey home, let fun begin!

So gather round, the blooms will share,
Tales of petals without a care.
Join their glee in nature's foam,
As every petal finds its home!

www.ingramcontent.com/pod-product-compliance
Lightning Source LLC
Chambersburg PA
CBHW051656160426
43209CB00004B/923